GRAPHIC SCIENCE

THE SURPRISING WORLD OF

BACTERIA

WITH *MAX AXIOM*
SUPER SCIENTIST

by Agnieszka Biskup

illustrated by Tod G. Smith

Consultant:
Dr. Beth Traxler
Associate Professor of Microbiology
University of Washington
Seattle, Washington

CAPSTONE PRESS
a capstone imprint

Graphic Library is published by Capstone Press,
1710 Roe Crest Drive, North Mankato, Minnesota 56003.
www.capstonepub.com

 Books published by Capstone Press are manufactured with paper
containing at least 10 percent post-consumer waste.

Library of Congress Cataloging-in-Publication Data
Biskup, Agnieszka.
    The surprising world of bacteria with Max Axiom, super scientist / by Agnieszka
Biskup ; illustrated by Tod G. Smith and Anne Timmons.
    p. cm. — (Graphic library. Graphic science)
    Summary: "In graphic novel format, follows Max Axiom as he explores the world of
bacteria" — Provided by publisher.
    Includes bibliographical references and index.
    ISBN 978-1-4296-3975-0 (library binding)
    ISBN 978-1-4296-4863-9 (paperback)
    1. Bacteria — Comic books, strips, etc. — Juvenile literature. I. Smith, Tod, ill.
II. Timmons, Anne, ill. III. Title.
QR74.8.B57 2010
579.3 — dc22   2009035303

Designer
Alison Thiele

Media Researcher
Wanda Winch

Cover Colorist
Krista Ward

Production Specialist
Laura Manthe

Colorist
Matt Webb

Editor
Anthony Wacholtz

Photo illustration credits: AVRDC - The World Vegetable Center, 19; Shutterstock/
Sebastian Kaulitzki, 9

Printed in the United States of America in North Mankato, Minnesota.
052012   006767R

TABLE OF CONTENTS

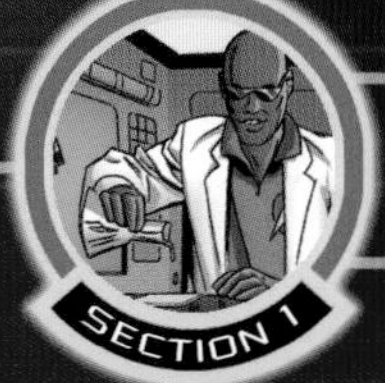
SECTION 1

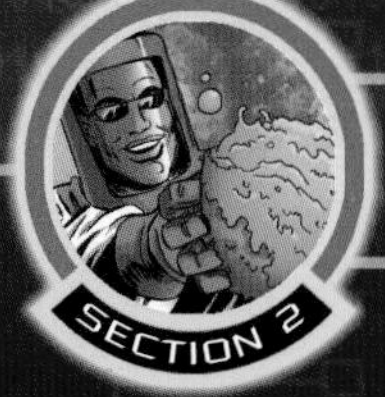
SECTION 2

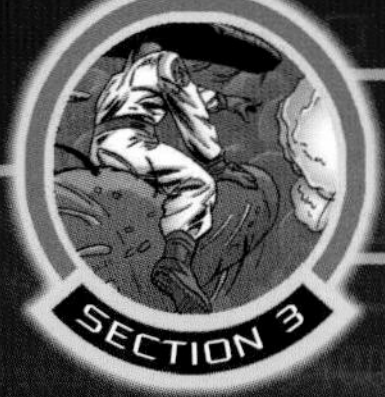
SECTION 3

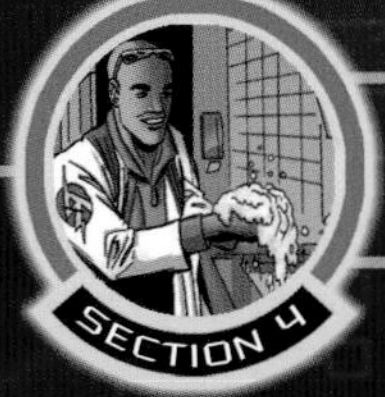
SECTION 4

SECTION 1 IT'S A SMALL WORLD

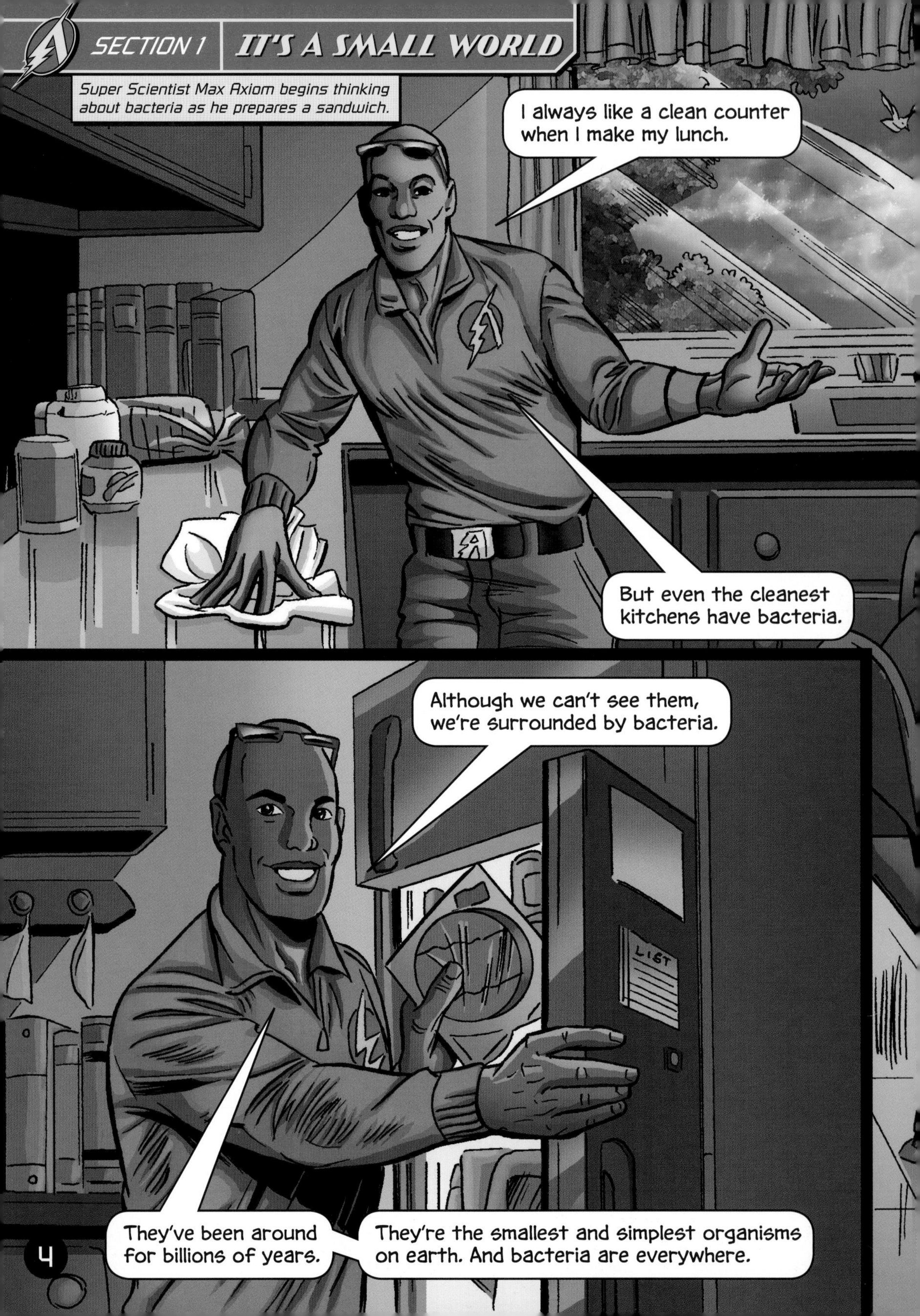

Super Scientist Max Axiom begins thinking about bacteria as he prepares a sandwich.
I always like a clean counter when I make my lunch.
But even the cleanest kitchens have bacteria.
Although we can't see them, we're surrounded by bacteria.
LIST
They've been around for billions of years.
They're the smallest and simplest organisms on earth. And bacteria are everywhere.

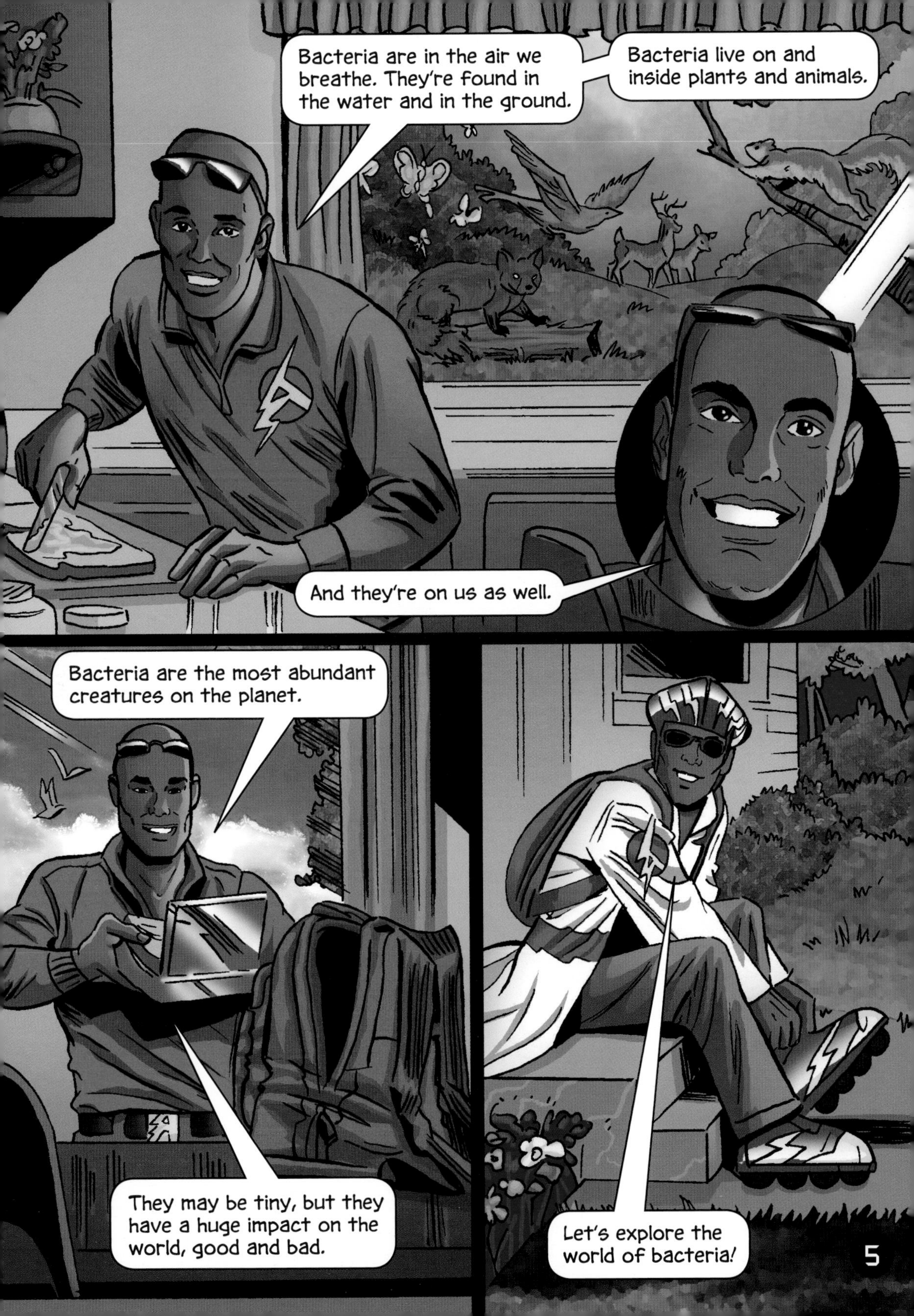
Bacteria are in the air we breathe. They're found in the water and in the ground.
Bacteria live on and inside plants and animals.
And they're on us as well.
Bacteria are the most abundant creatures on the planet.
They may be tiny, but they have a huge impact on the world, good and bad.
Let's explore the world of bacteria!

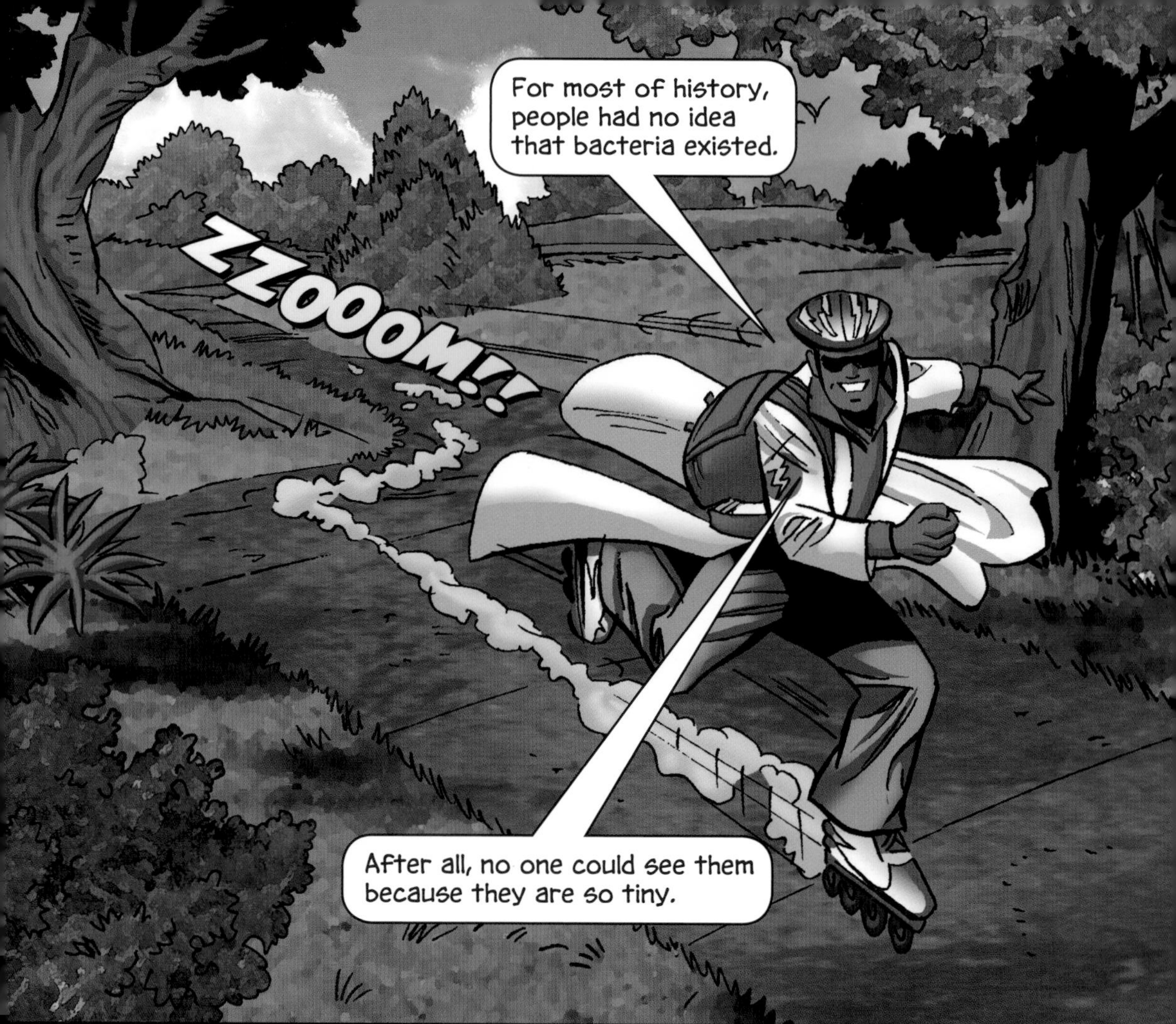

For most of history, people had no idea that bacteria existed.
ZZOOOM!!
After all, no one could see them because they are so tiny.

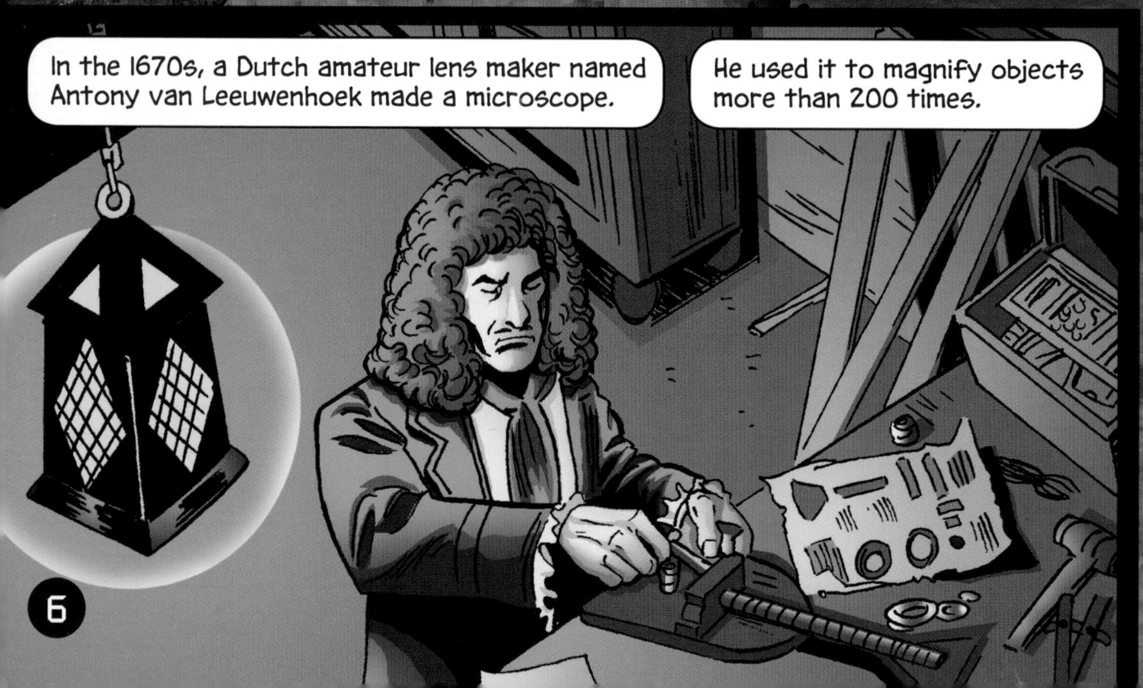

In the 1670s, a Dutch amateur lens maker named Antony van Leeuwenhoek made a microscope.
He used it to magnify objects more than 200 times.

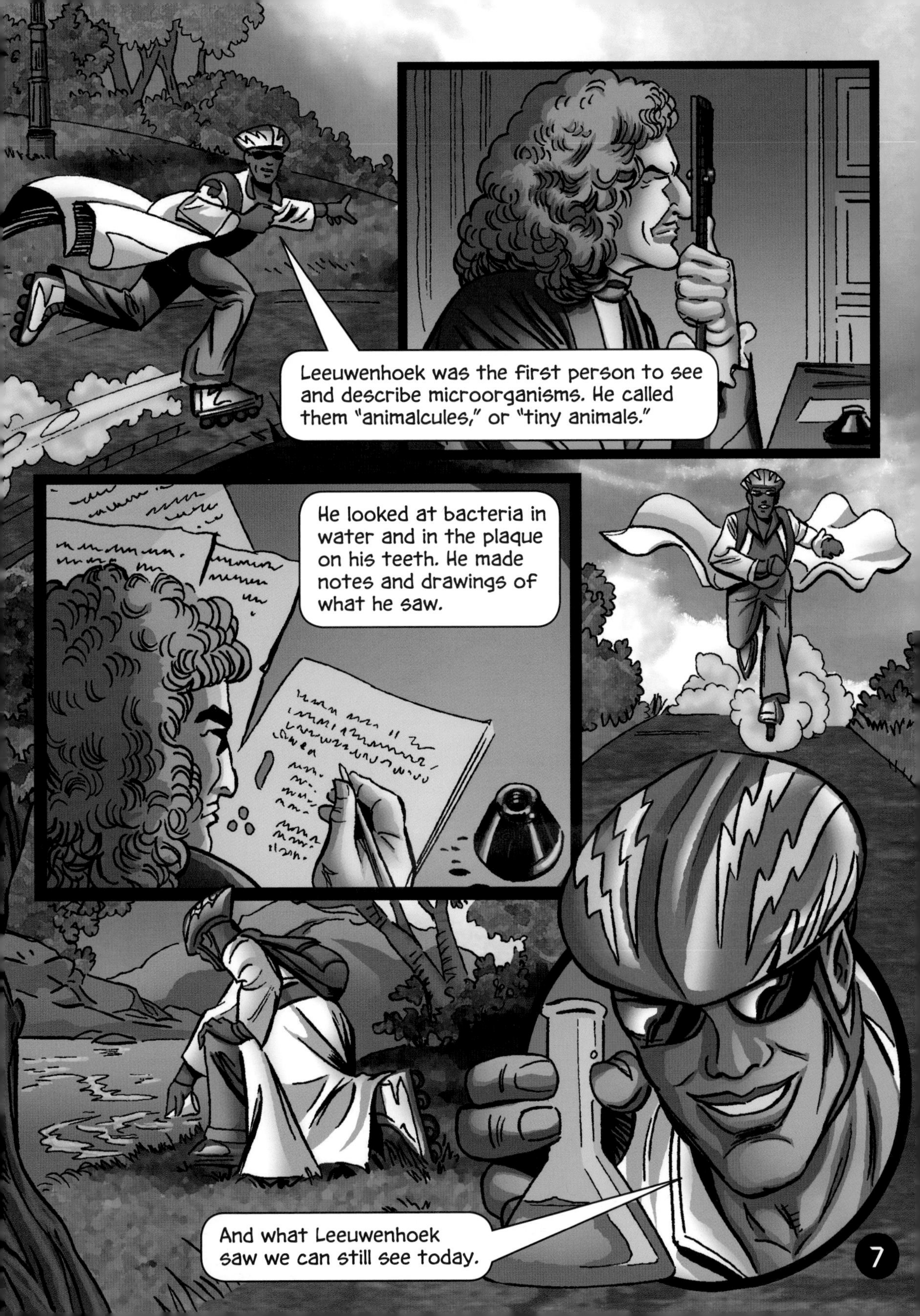
Leeuwenhoek was the first person to see and describe microorganisms. He called them "animalcules," or "tiny animals."
He looked at bacteria in water and in the plaque on his teeth. He made notes and drawings of what he saw.
And what Leeuwenhoek saw we can still see today.

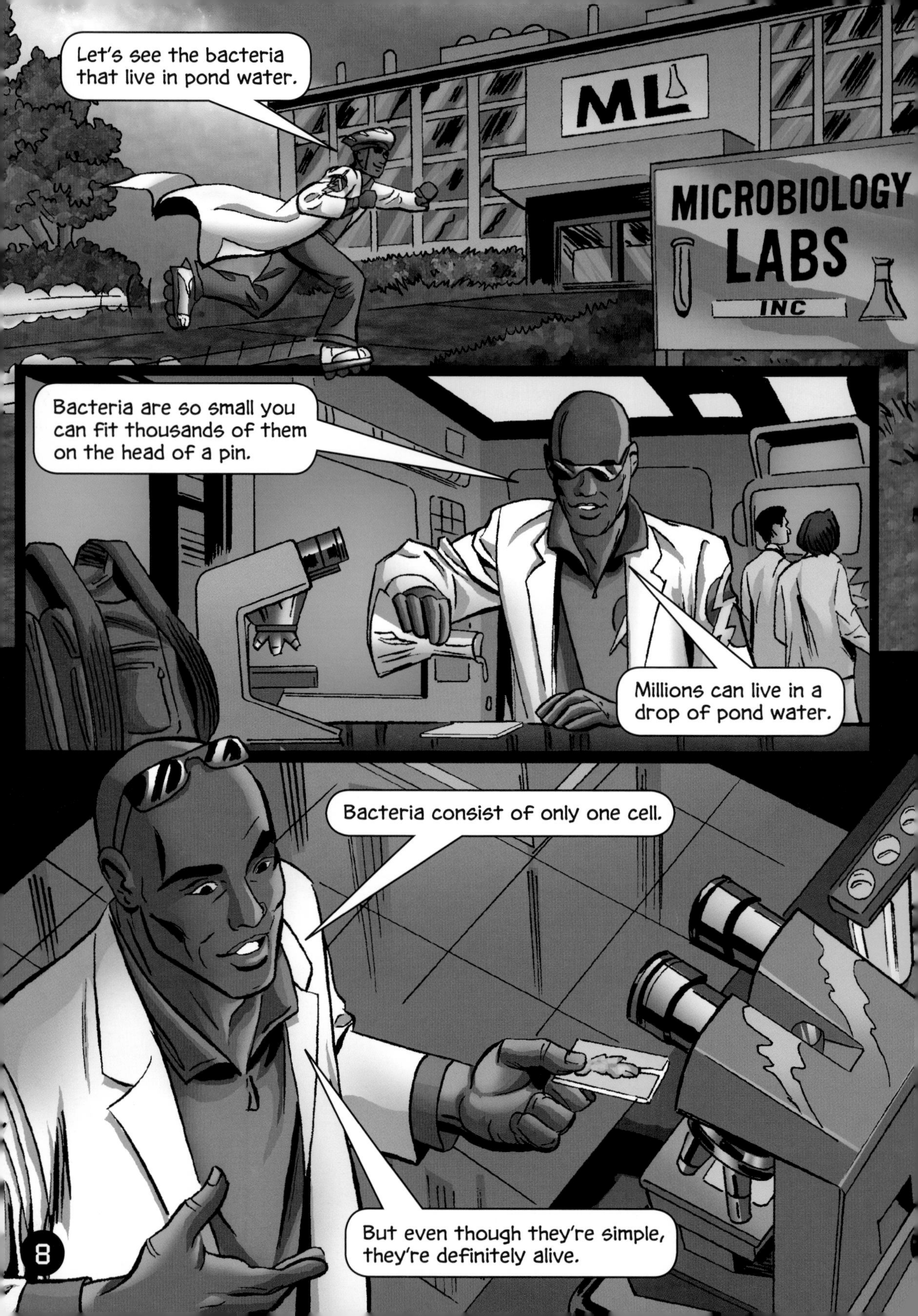

Let's see the bacteria that live in pond water.
ML
MICROBIOLOGY LABS INC
Bacteria are so small you can fit thousands of them on the head of a pin.
Millions can live in a drop of pond water.
Bacteria consist of only one cell.
But even though they're simple, they're definitely alive.

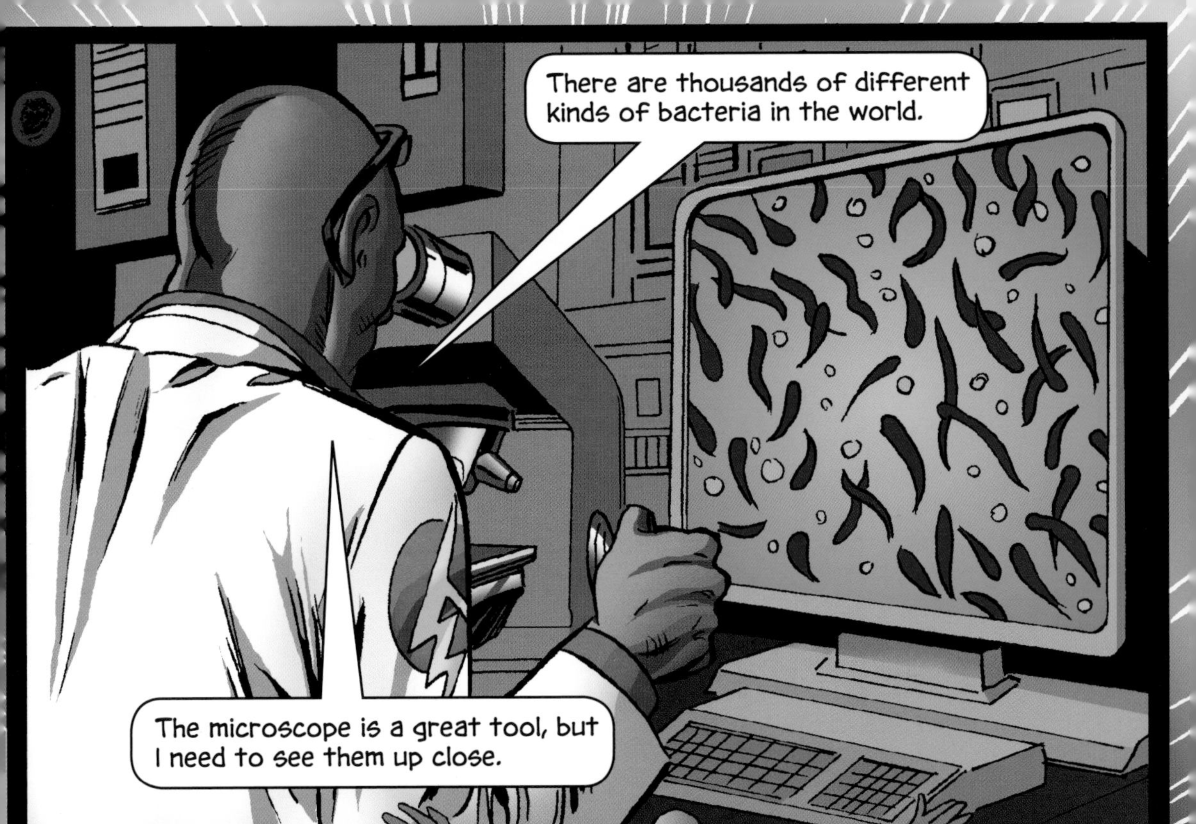
There are thousands of different kinds of bacteria in the world.
The microscope is a great tool, but I need to see them up close.
To see bacteria firsthand, I've got to shrink down to their microscopic size.

CELLS EVERYWHERE

ACCESS GRANTED: MAX AXIOM

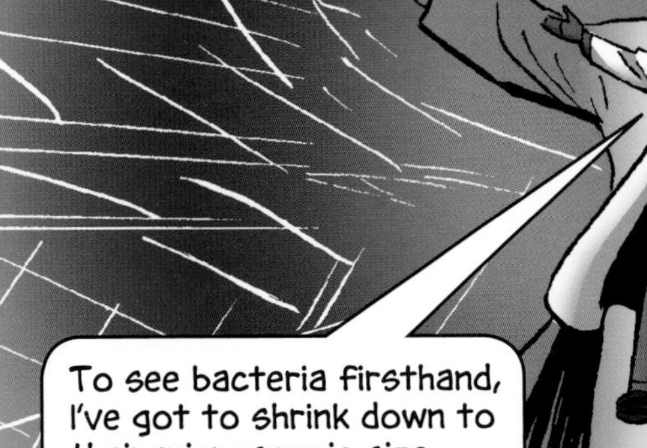

Cells are the basic unit of all living things. Every living thing is made up of one or more cells. Unlike bacteria, our bodies are made up of trillions of cells.

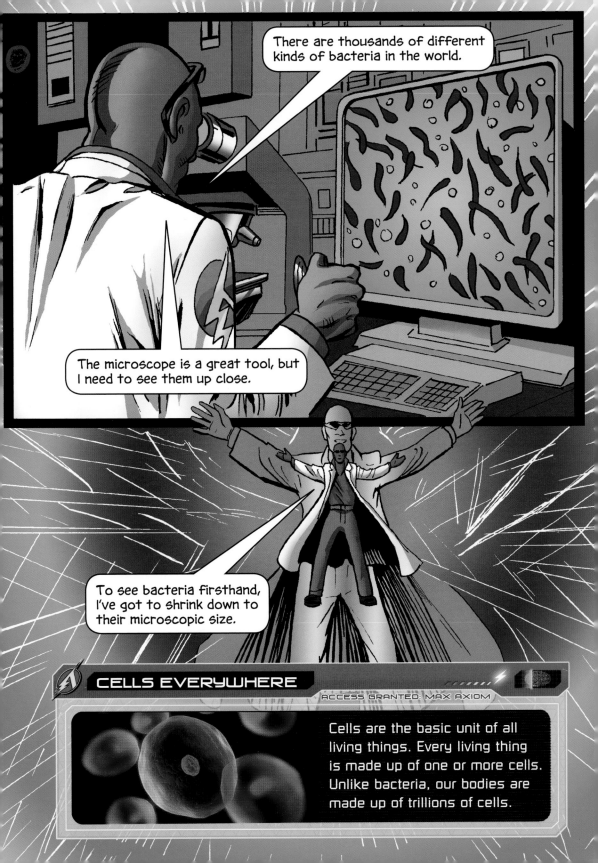

SECTION 2 | BACTERIA UP CLOSE

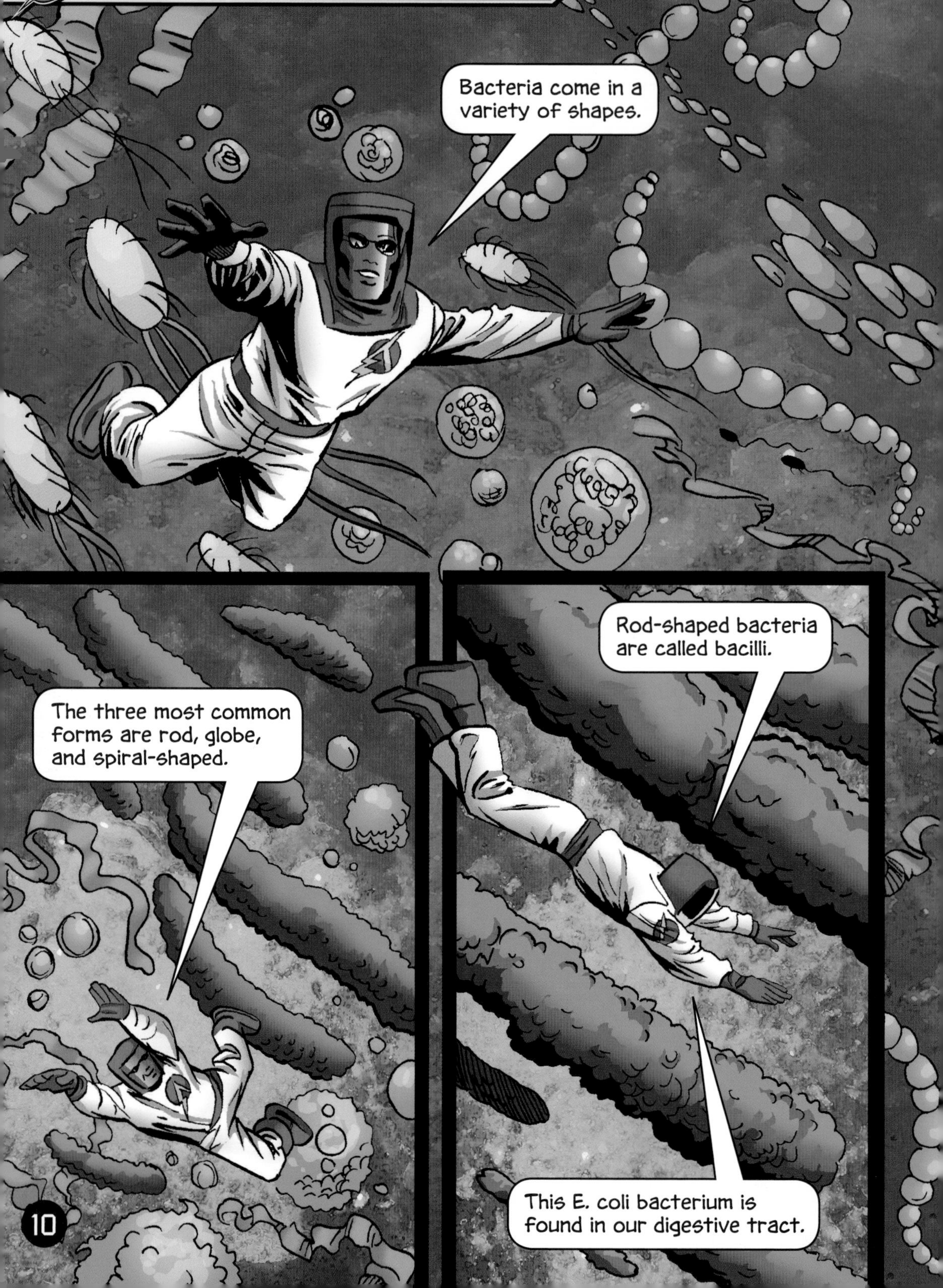

Bacteria come in a variety of shapes.
The three most common forms are rod, globe, and spiral-shaped.
Rod-shaped bacteria are called bacilli.
This E. coli bacterium is found in our digestive tract.

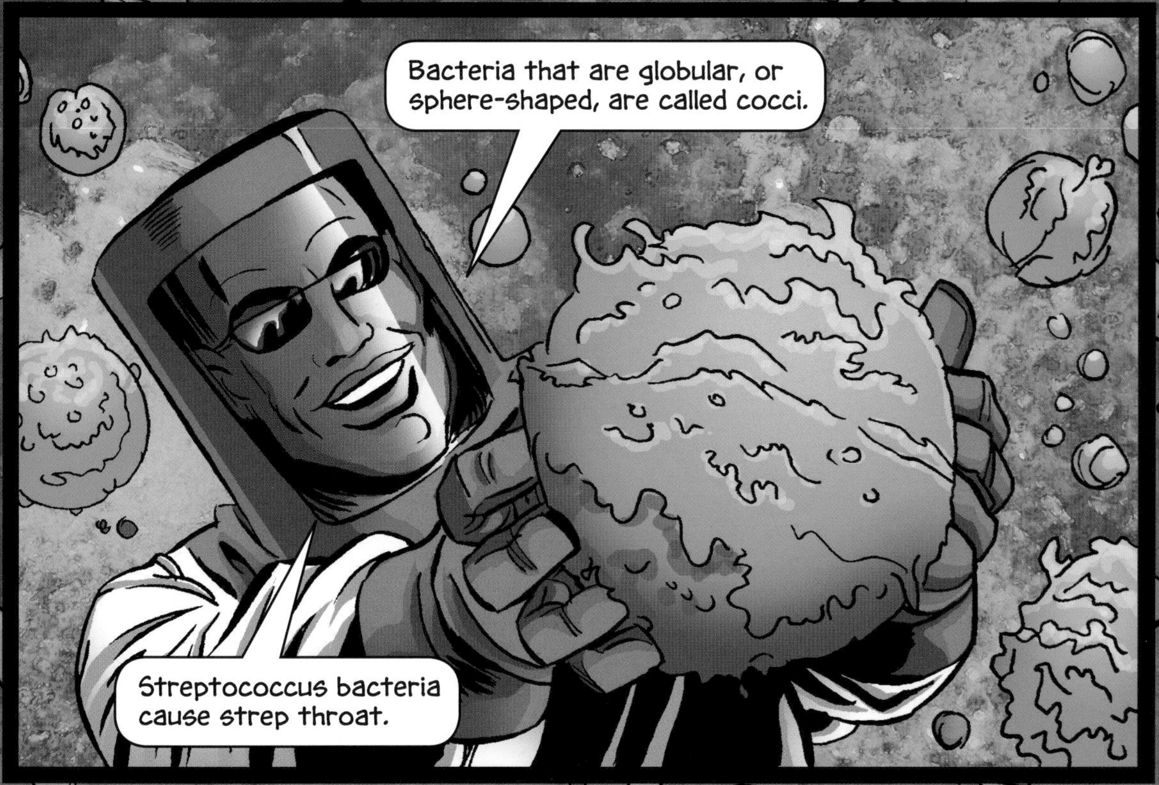
Bacteria that are globular, or sphere-shaped, are called cocci.
Streptococcus bacteria cause strep throat.

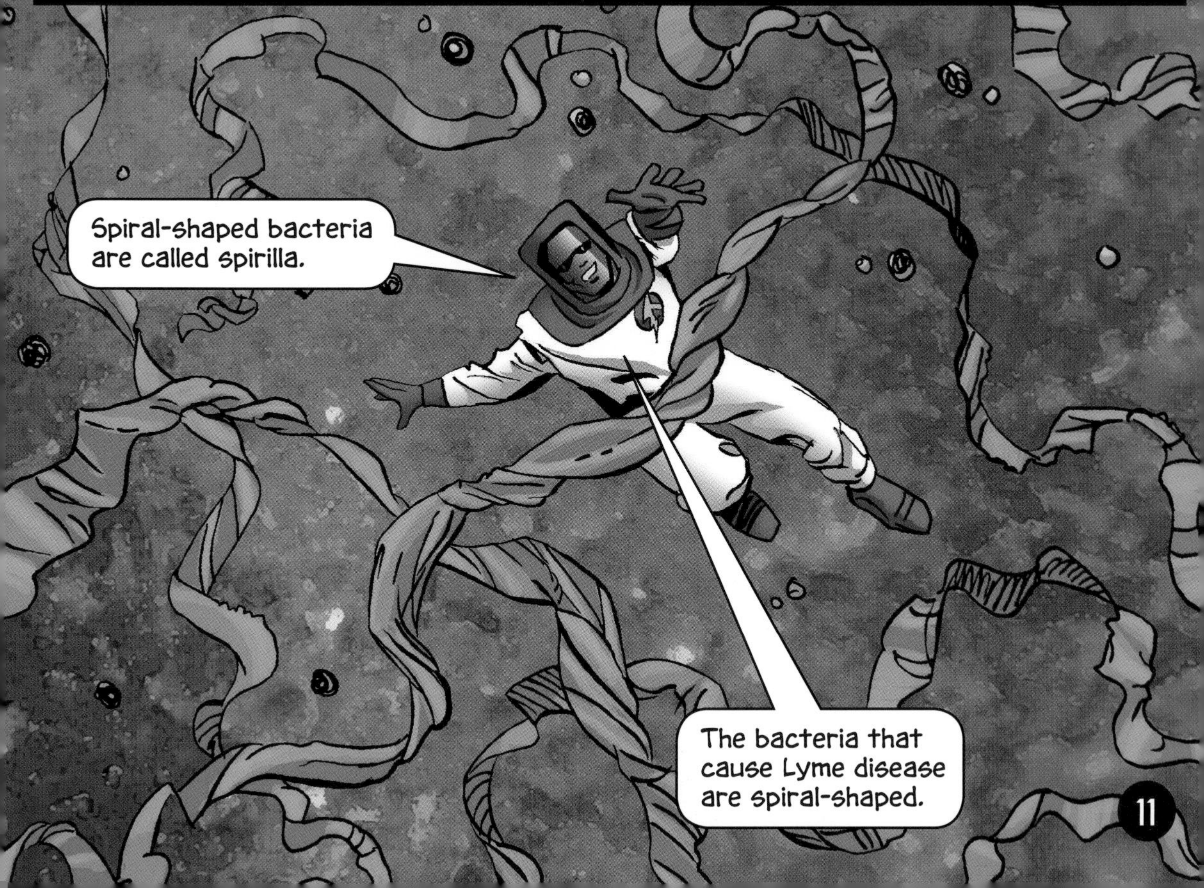
Spiral-shaped bacteria are called spirilla.
The bacteria that cause Lyme disease are spiral-shaped.

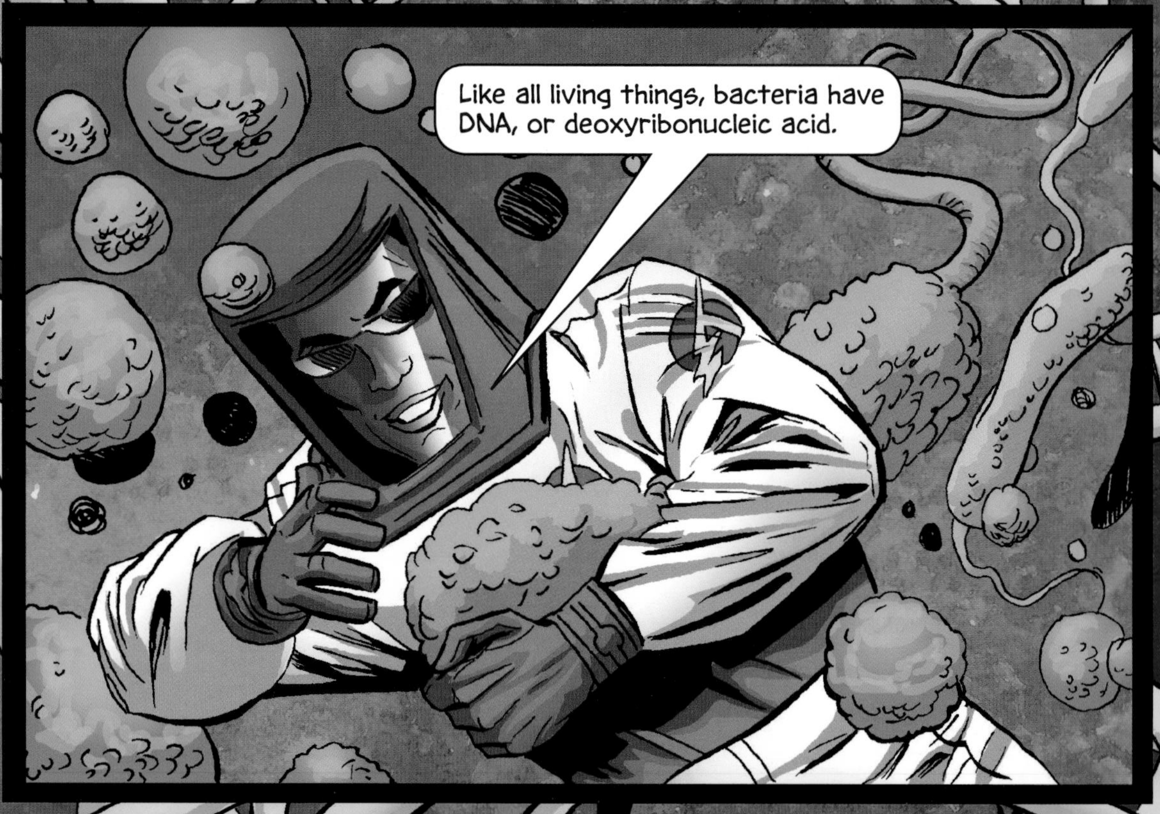
Like all living things, bacteria have DNA, or deoxyribonucleic acid.

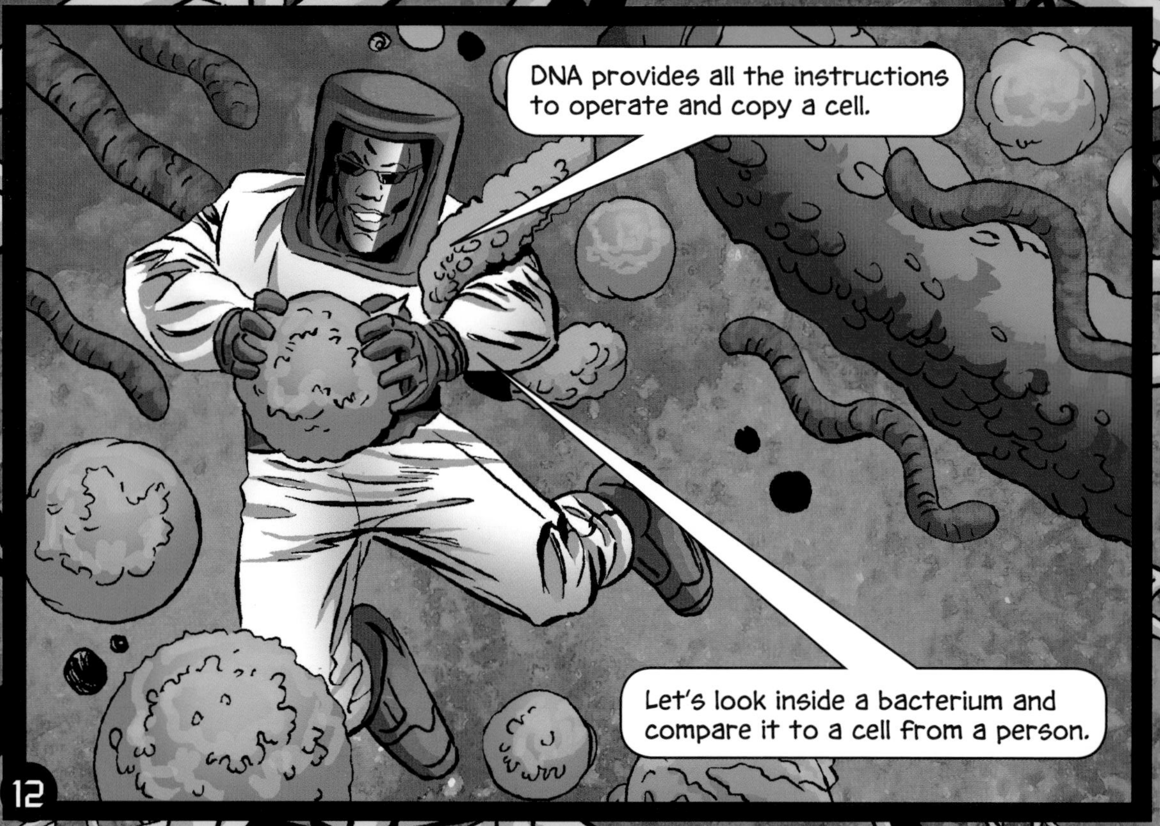
DNA provides all the instructions to operate and copy a cell.
Let's look inside a bacterium and compare it to a cell from a person.

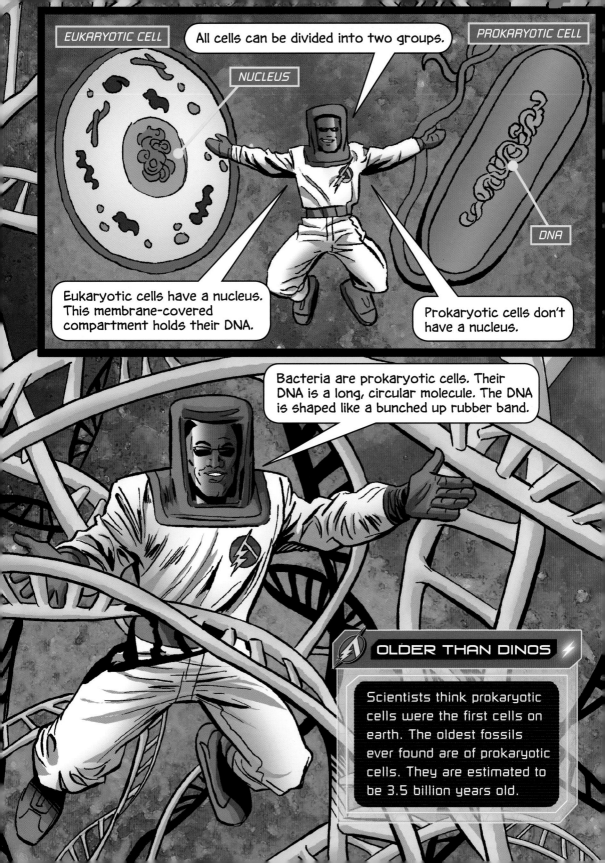

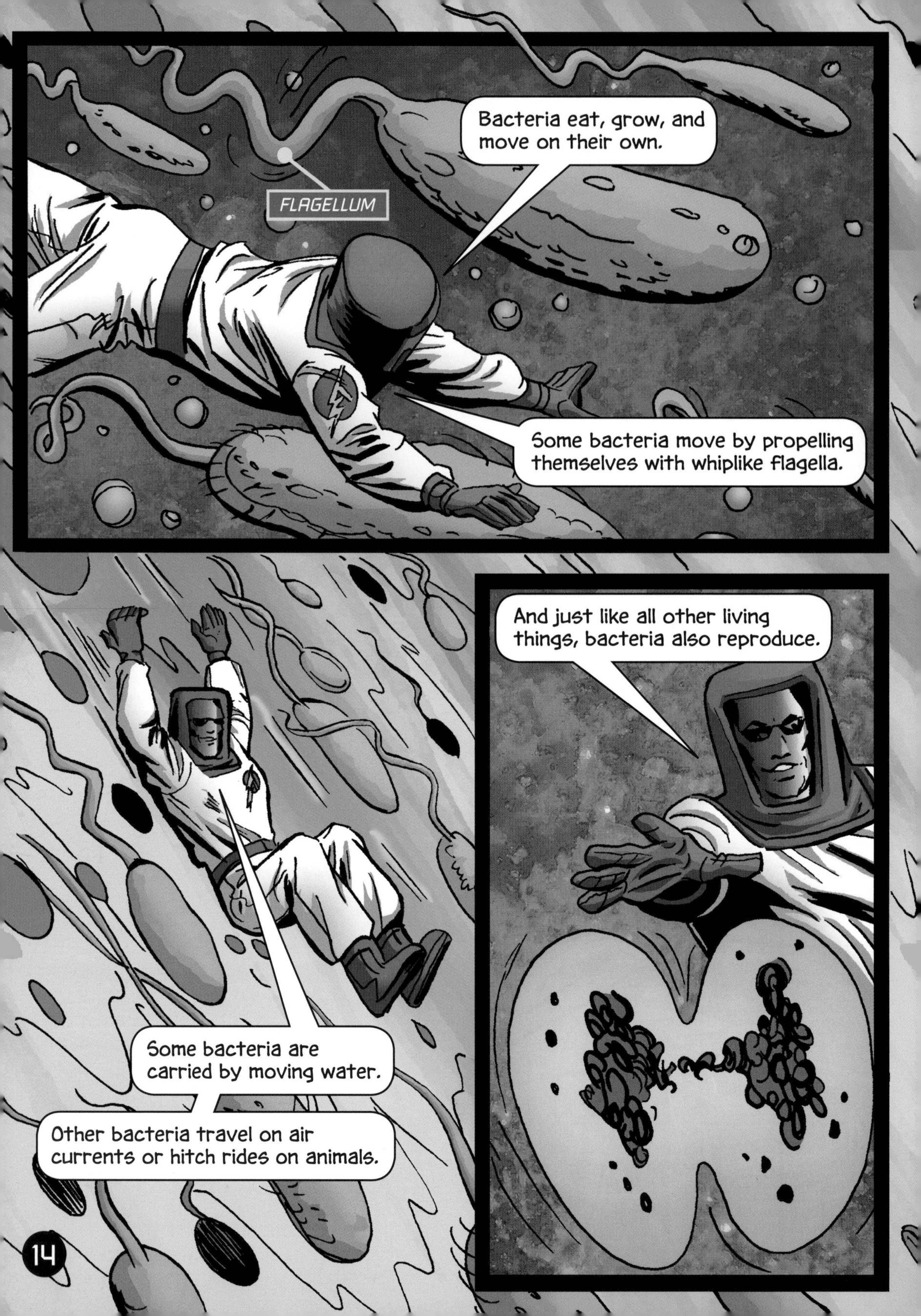
Bacteria eat, grow, and move on their own.
FLAGELLUM
Some bacteria move by propelling themselves with whiplike flagella.
Some bacteria are carried by moving water.
Other bacteria travel on air currents or hitch rides on animals.
And just like all other living things, bacteria also reproduce.

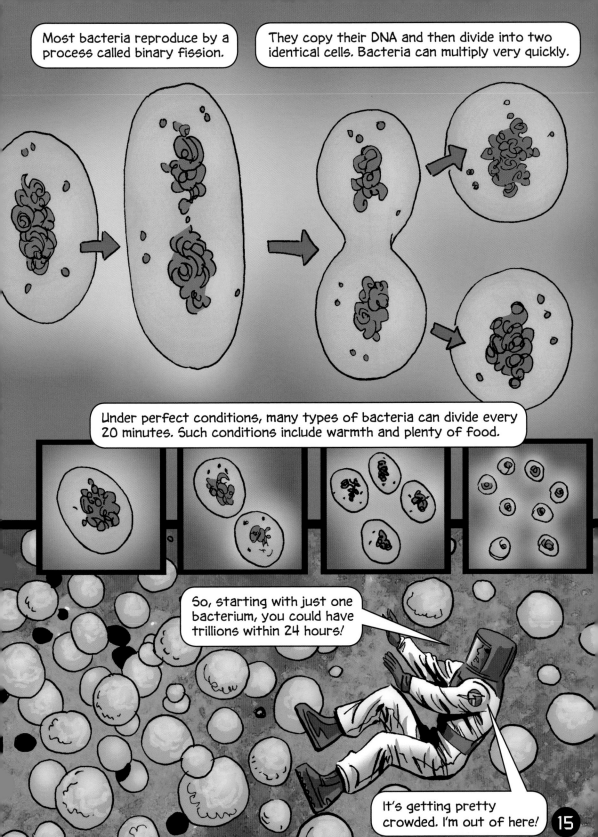

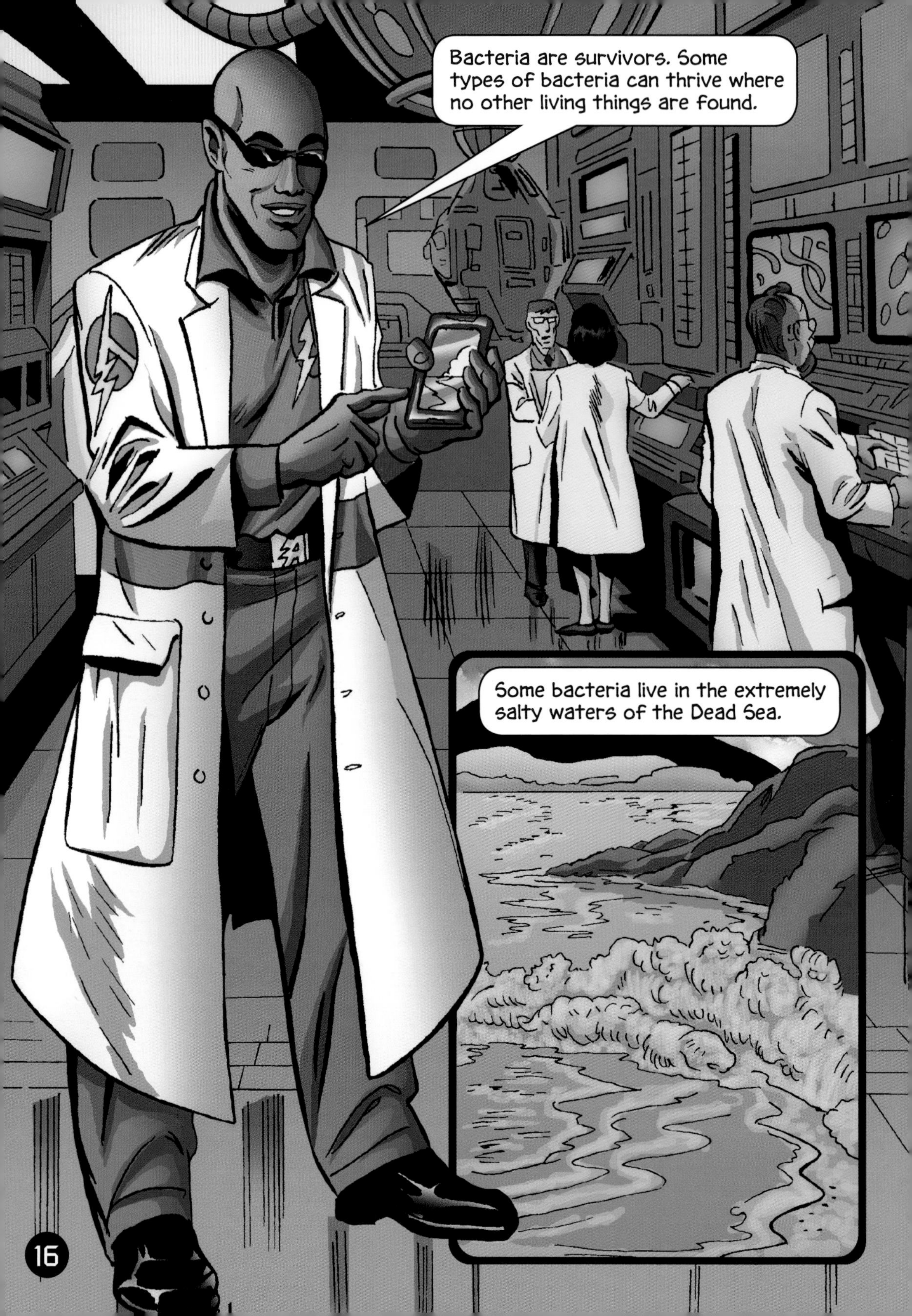

Bacteria are survivors. Some types of bacteria can thrive where no other living things are found.
Some bacteria live in the extremely salty waters of the Dead Sea.

Bacteria have been found deep under Antarctic ice.

They live in near-boiling temperatures at the hot springs of Yellowstone National Park.

Bacteria have even been found in clouds high above earth's surface.

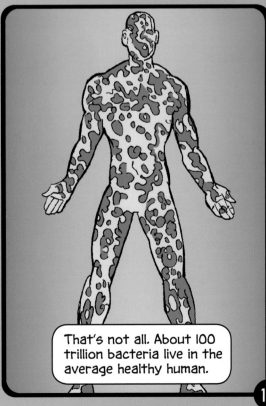

That's not all. About 100 trillion bacteria live in the average healthy human.

SECTION 3 FRIENDS AND FOES

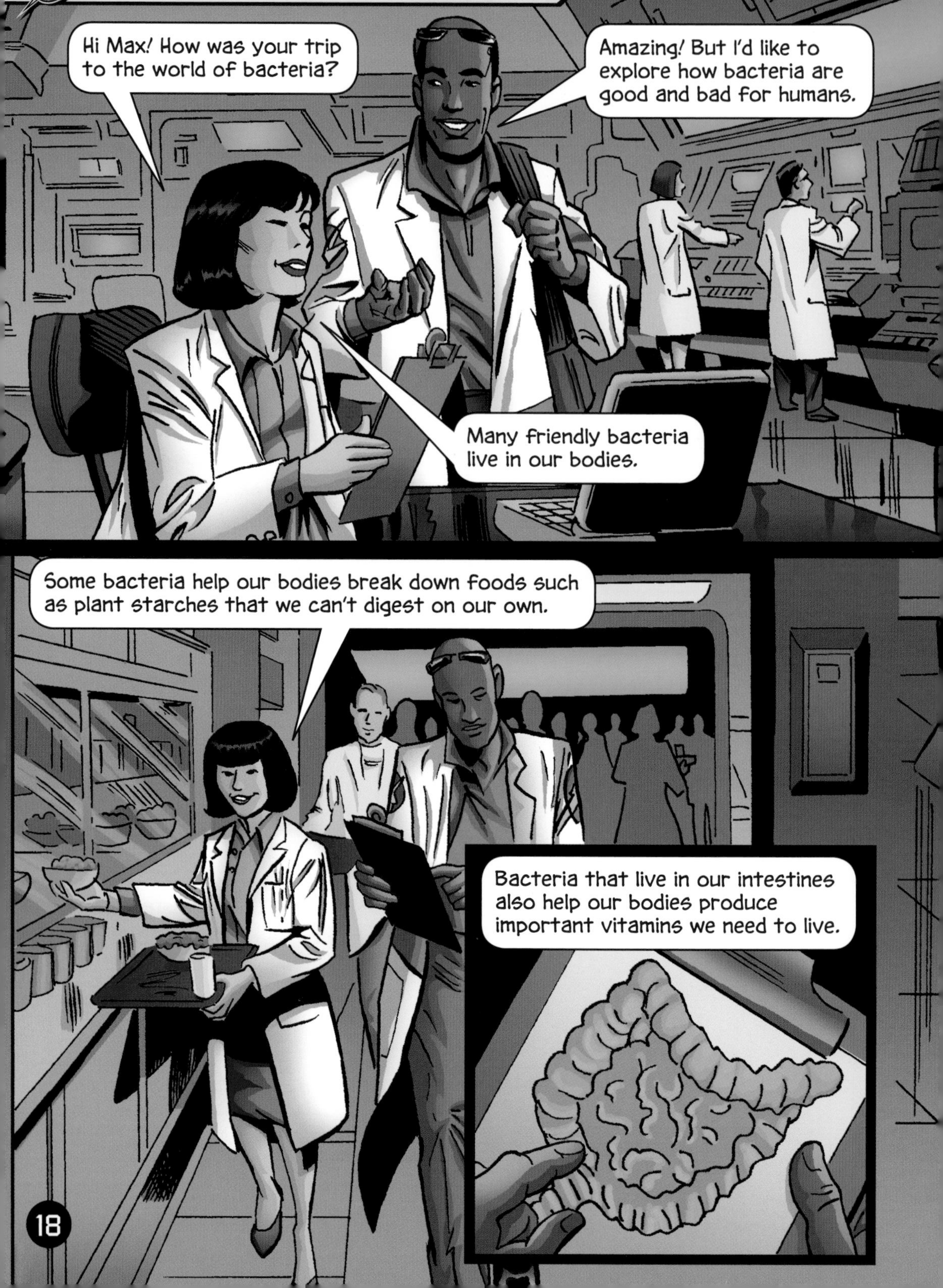

Hi Max! How was your trip to the world of bacteria?
Amazing! But I'd like to explore how bacteria are good and bad for humans.
Many friendly bacteria live in our bodies.
Some bacteria help our bodies break down foods such as plant starches that we can't digest on our own.
Bacteria that live in our intestines also help our bodies produce important vitamins we need to live.

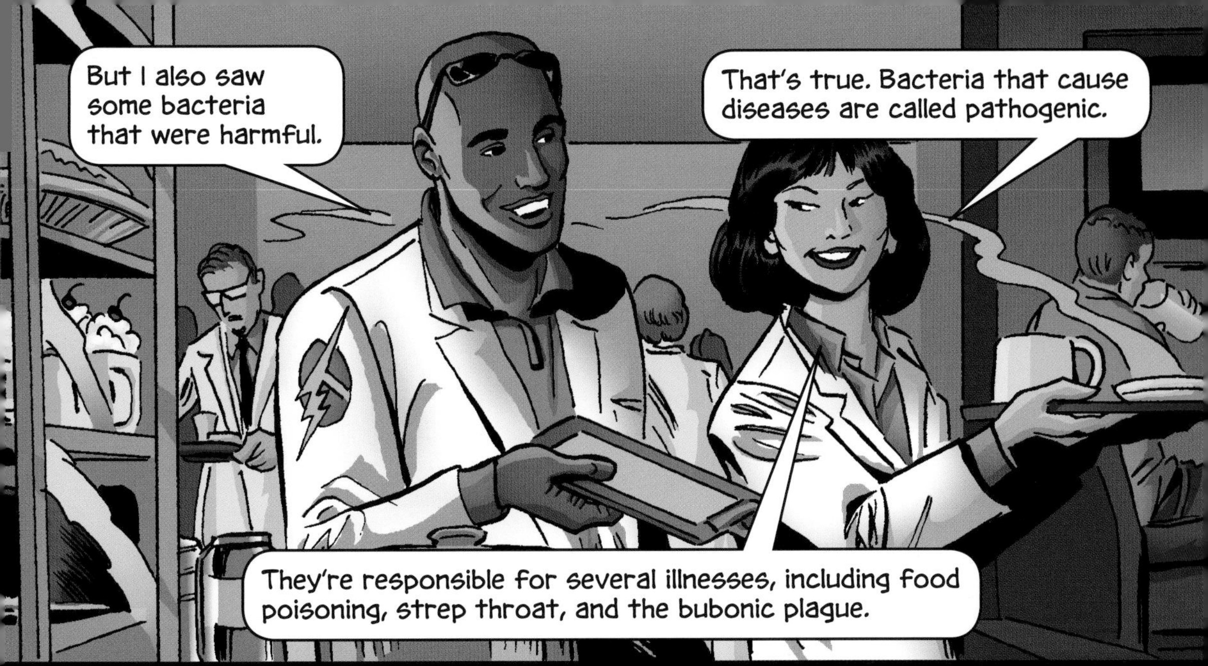
But I also saw some bacteria that were harmful.
That's true. Bacteria that cause diseases are called pathogenic.
They're responsible for several illnesses, including food poisoning, strep throat, and the bubonic plague.

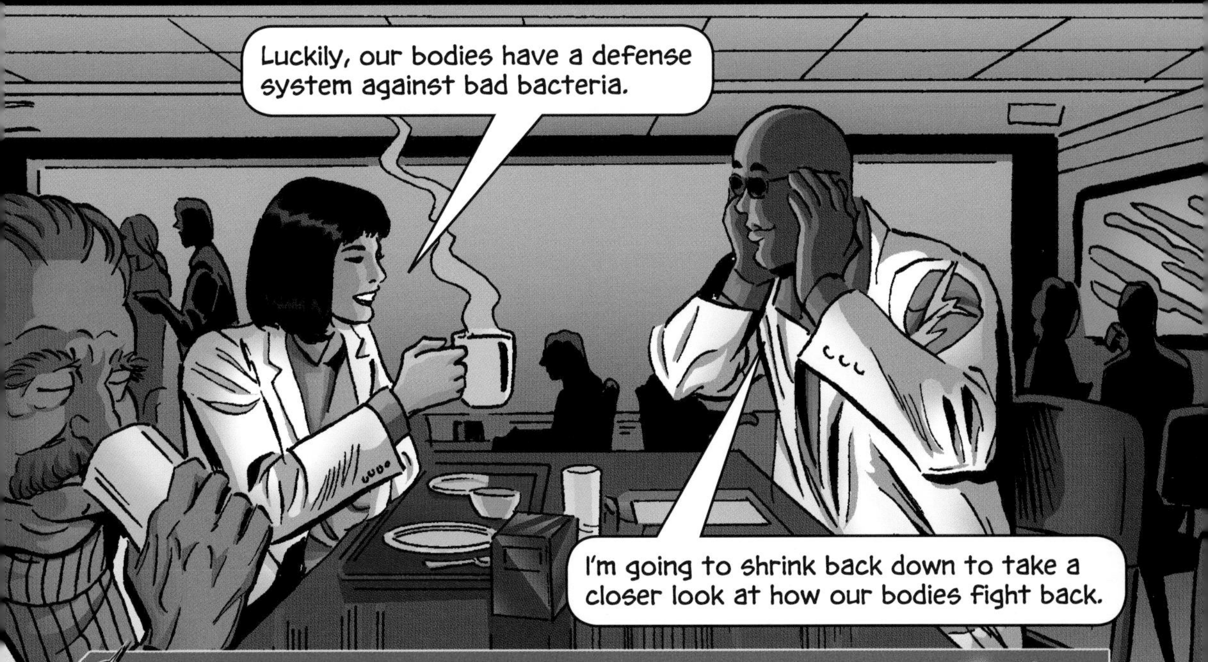
Luckily, our bodies have a defense system against bad bacteria.
I'm going to shrink back down to take a closer look at how our bodies fight back.

BAD BACTERIA

ACCESS GRANTED: MAX AXIOM

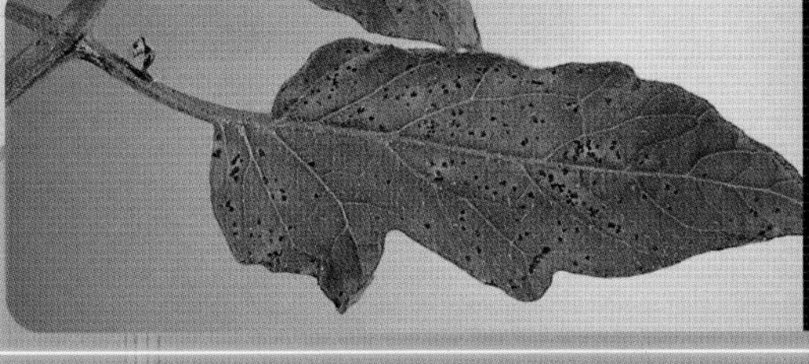

Pathogenic bacteria can attack plants, animals, fungi, and even other bacteria. Pathogenic bacteria can create holes in leaves by releasing toxins that damage cells.

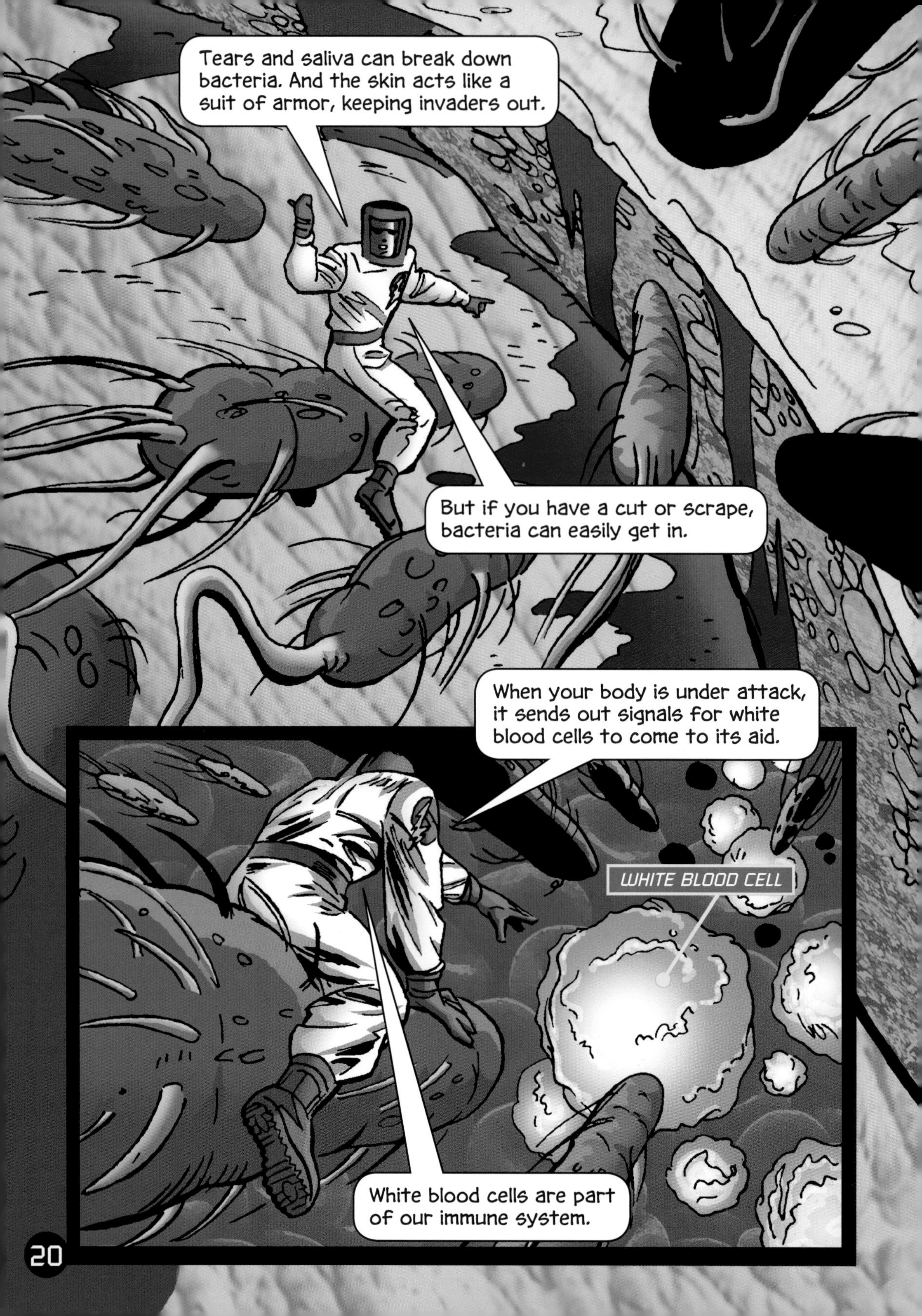
Tears and saliva can break down bacteria. And the skin acts like a suit of armor, keeping invaders out.
But if you have a cut or scrape, bacteria can easily get in.
When your body is under attack, it sends out signals for white blood cells to come to its aid.
WHITE BLOOD CELL
White blood cells are part of our immune system.

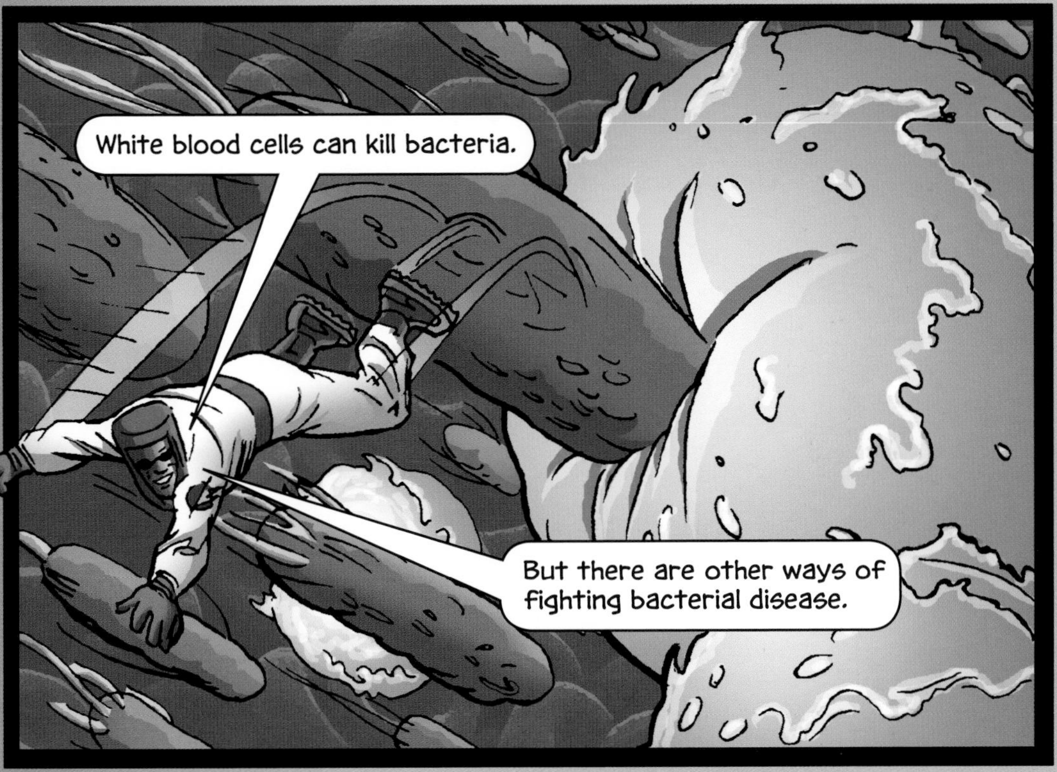
White blood cells can kill bacteria.
But there are other ways of fighting bacterial disease.

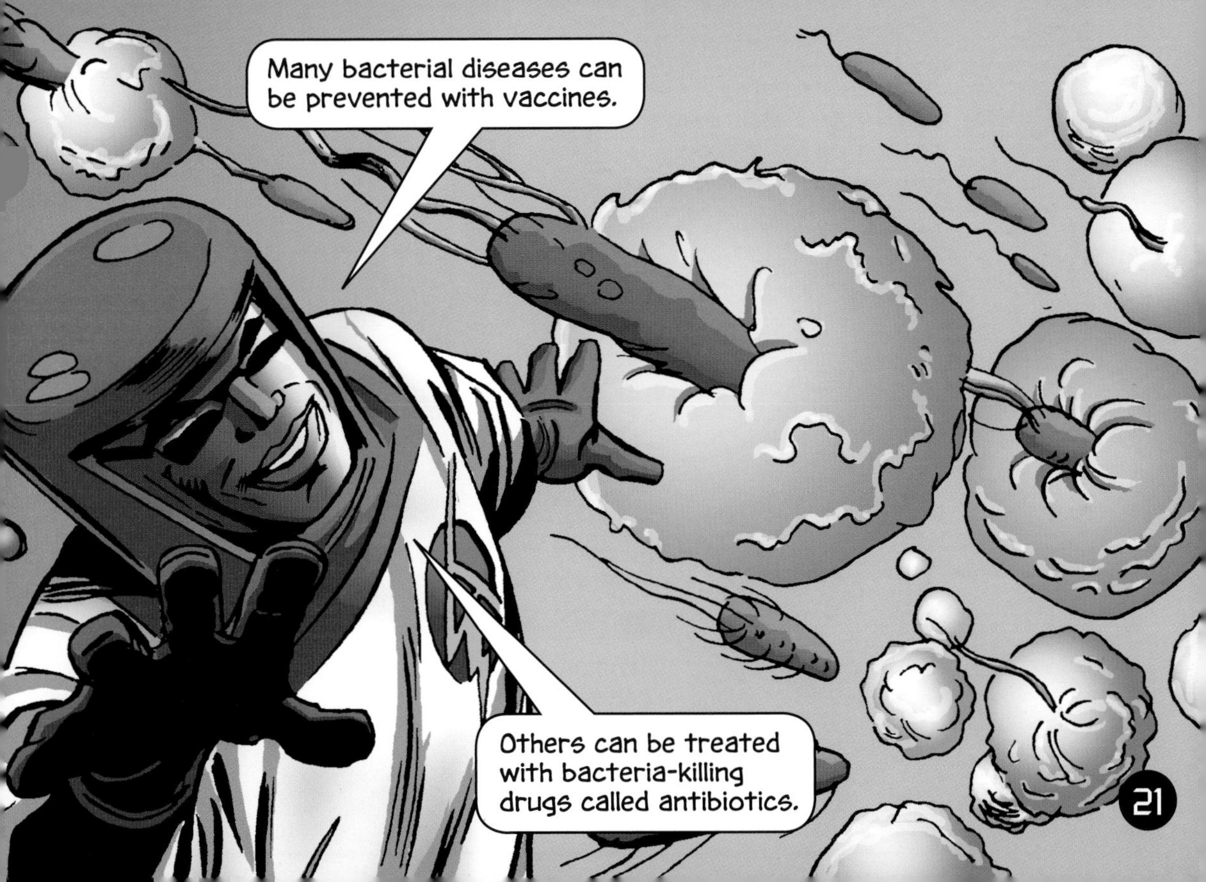
Many bacterial diseases can be prevented with vaccines.
Others can be treated with bacteria-killing drugs called antibiotics.

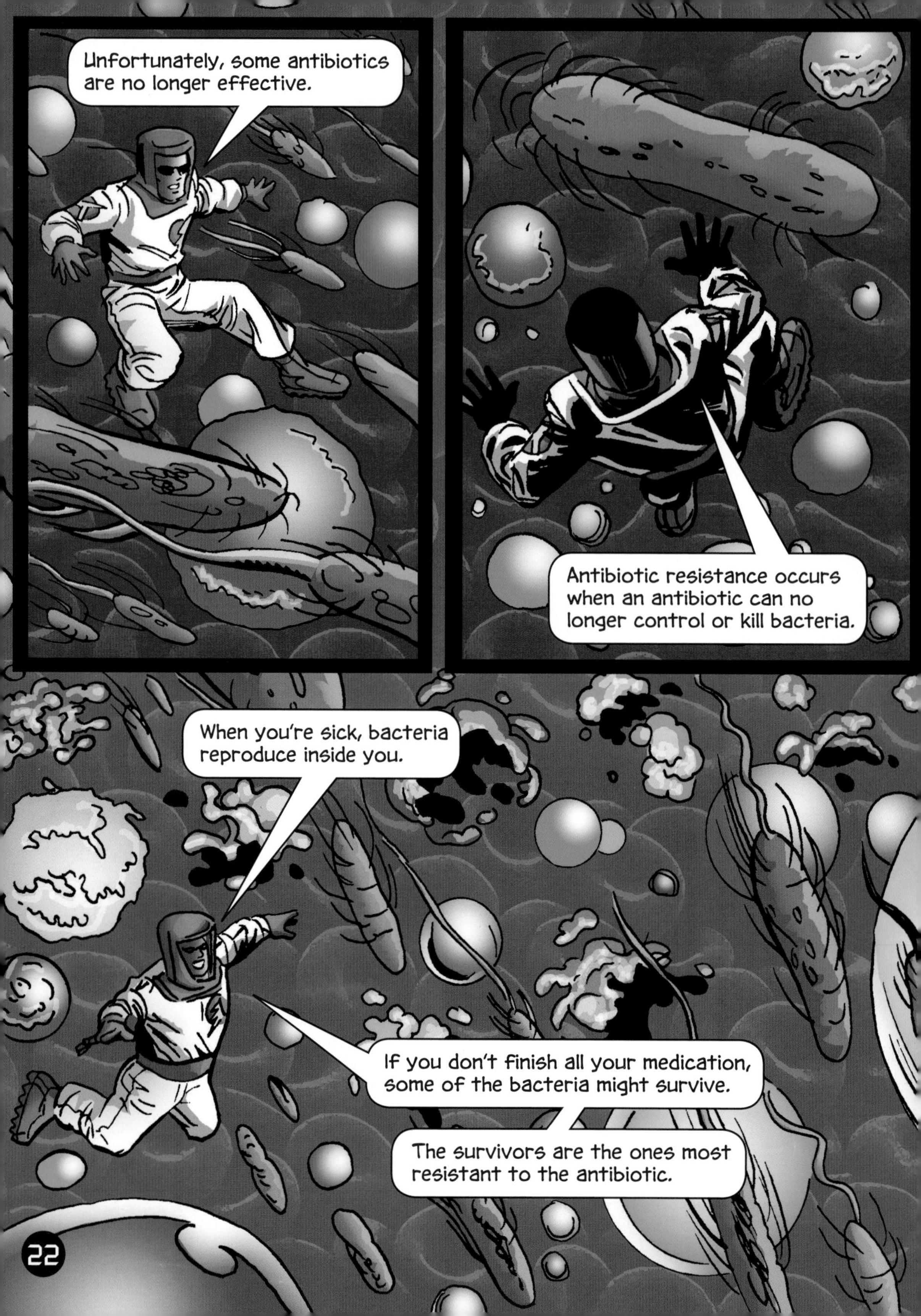

Unfortunately, some antibiotics are no longer effective.
Antibiotic resistance occurs when an antibiotic can no longer control or kill bacteria.
When you're sick, bacteria reproduce inside you.
If you don't finish all your medication, some of the bacteria might survive.
The survivors are the ones most resistant to the antibiotic.

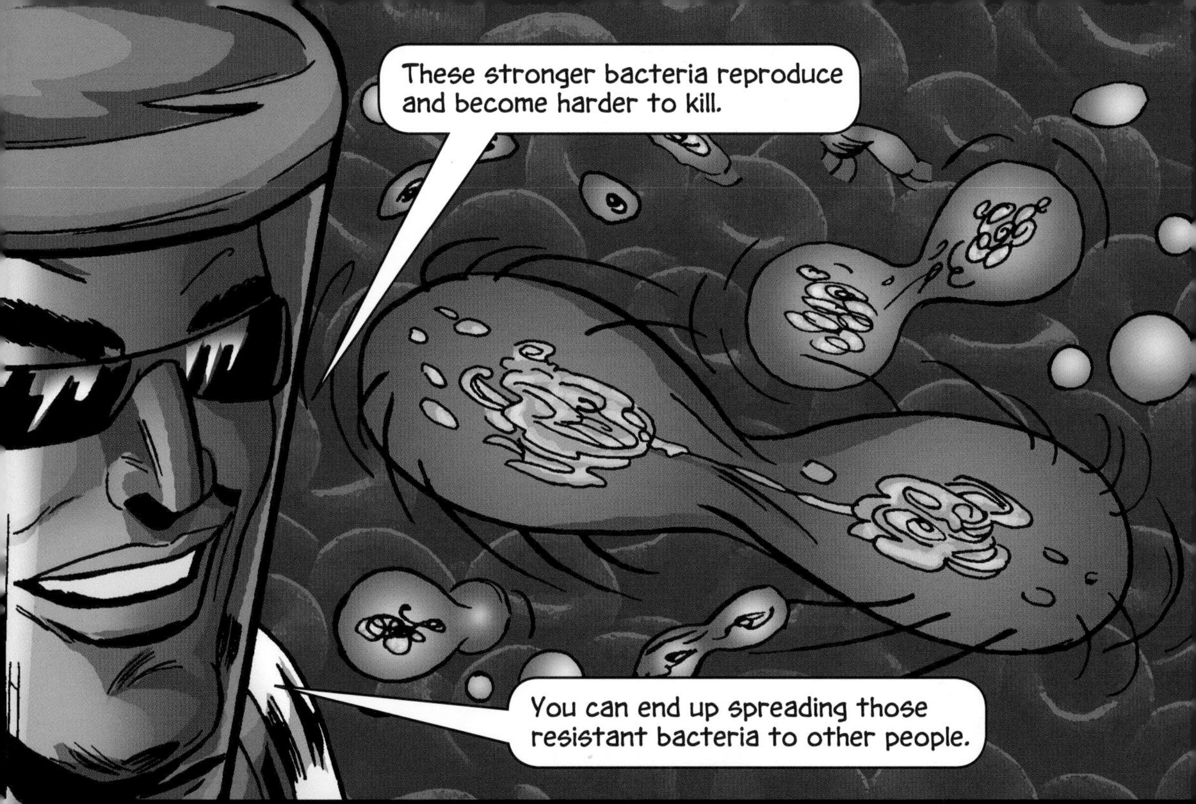
These stronger bacteria reproduce and become harder to kill.
You can end up spreading those resistant bacteria to other people.

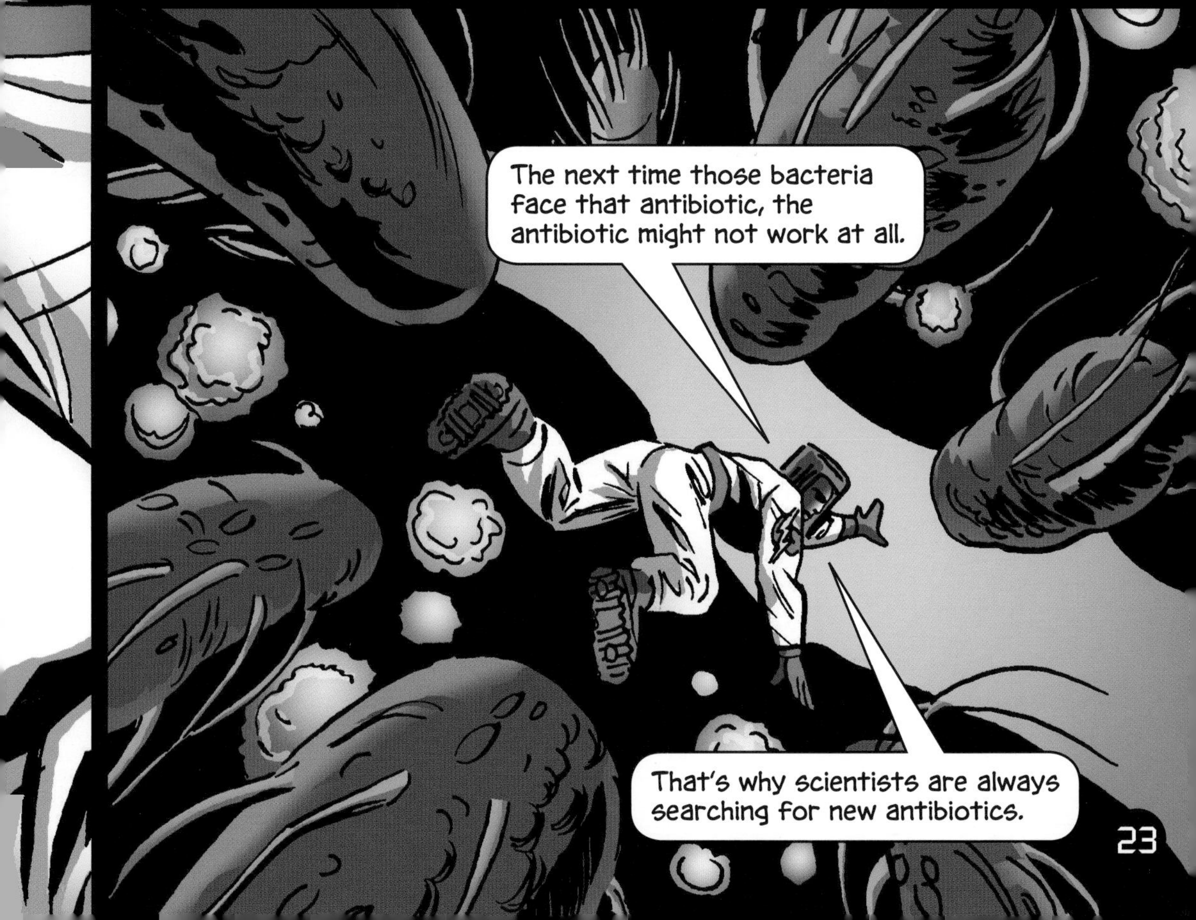
The next time those bacteria face that antibiotic, the antibiotic might not work at all.
That's why scientists are always searching for new antibiotics.

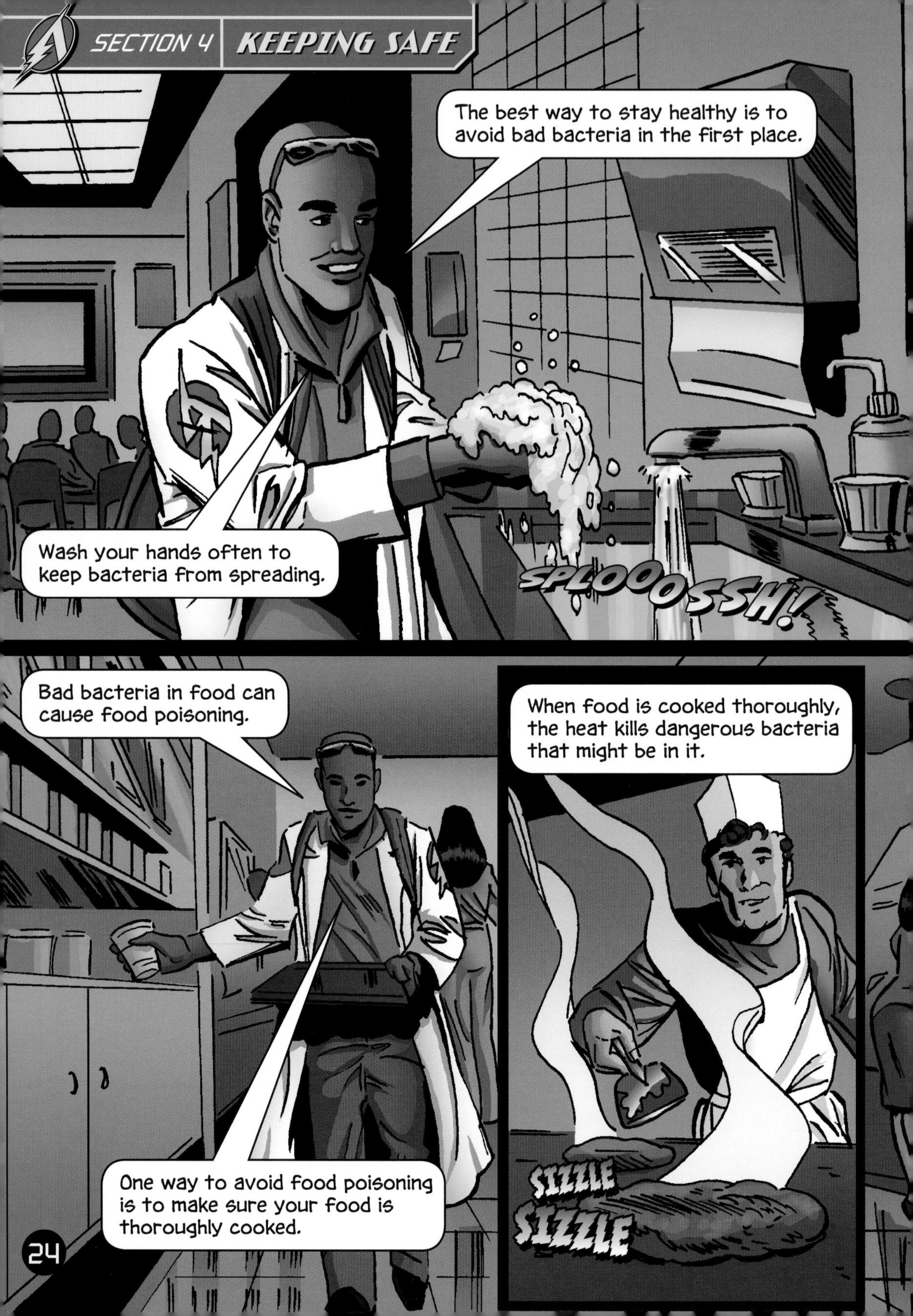
The best way to stay healthy is to avoid bad bacteria in the first place.
Wash your hands often to keep bacteria from spreading.
SPLOOOSSH!
Bad bacteria in food can cause food poisoning.
One way to avoid food poisoning is to make sure your food is thoroughly cooked.
When food is cooked thoroughly, the heat kills dangerous bacteria that might be in it.
SIZZLE
SIZZLE

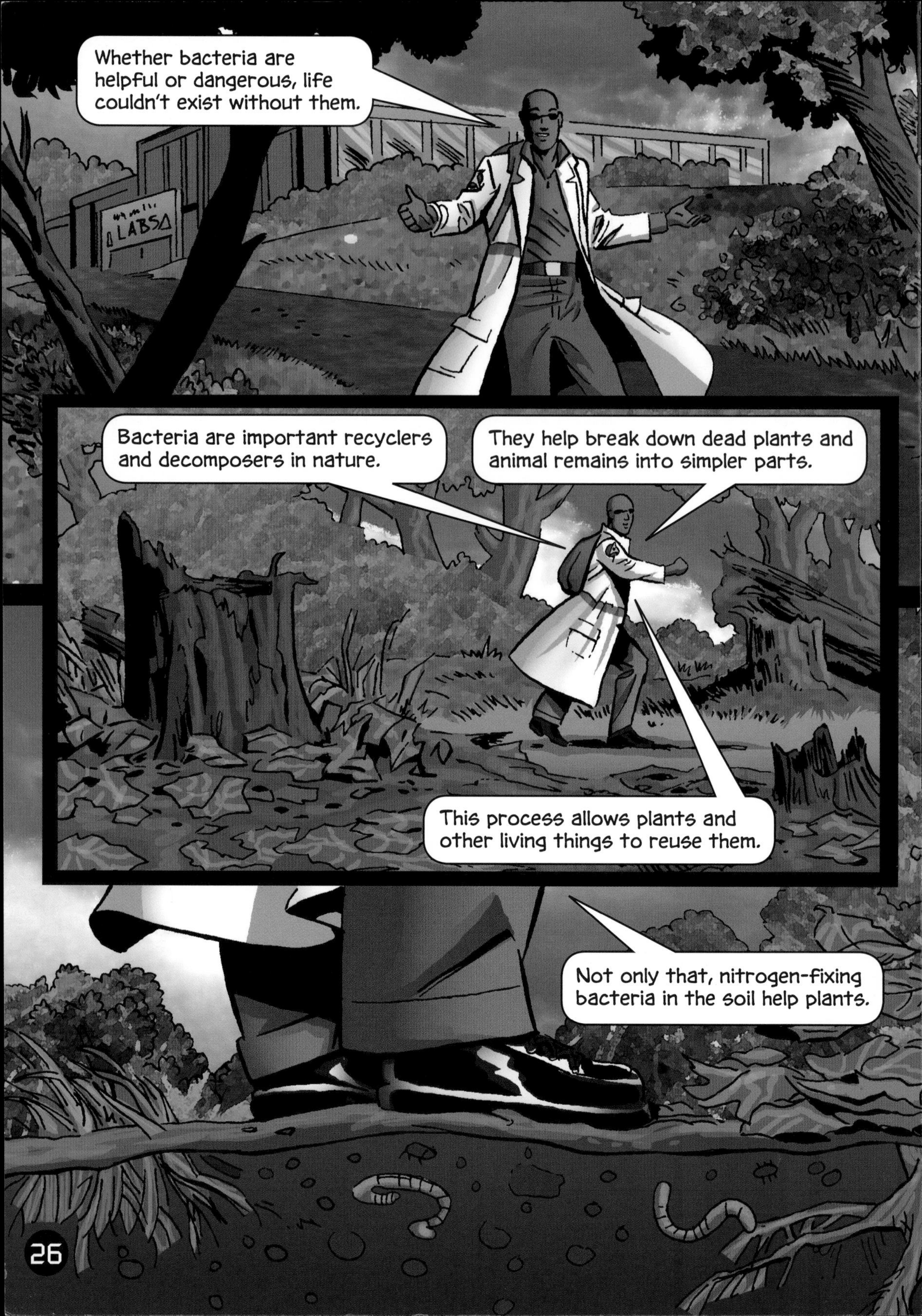

Whether bacteria are helpful or dangerous, life couldn't exist without them.
LABS
Bacteria are important recyclers and decomposers in nature.
They help break down dead plants and animal remains into simpler parts.
This process allows plants and other living things to reuse them.
Not only that, nitrogen-fixing bacteria in the soil help plants.

MORE ABOUT BACTERIA

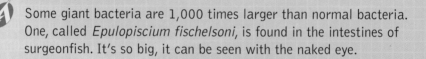

Some giant bacteria are 1,000 times larger than normal bacteria. One, called *Epulopiscium fischelsoni*, is found in the intestines of surgeonfish. It's so big, it can be seen with the naked eye.

Anaerobic bacteria don't need oxygen to live. Anaerobic bacteria live in soil and even inside our bodies. They're mostly harmless. But if they travel to a part of the body where they don't belong, they can cause serious illness and disease.

In 1928, Alexander Fleming discovered that a type of common mold could kill pathogenic bacteria. He isolated the bacteria-killing chemical from the mold and called it penicillin. It was the first antibiotic ever discovered.

Bacteria that live in the stomachs of cows and other cud-chewing animals help them digest tough plants and grasses.

Botulinum toxin, a poison produced by *Clostridium botulinum* bacteria, is one of the most deadly naturally occurring substances known. Despite this fact, doctors use very small amounts of the toxin to treat some medical conditions. It is best known today for its use as Botox. It is injected into the face where it paralyzes muscles, helping reduce lines and wrinkles.

Vaccines have been made for bacterial diseases such as whooping cough, diphtheria, tetanus, and Lyme disease.

E. coli move by whipping their flagella. They can travel a distance equal to 25 times their length in only a second.

 Bacteria have changed the face of the planet. About two or three billion years ago, bacteria that used sunlight for energy emerged. They also gave off oxygen in the process. Thanks to bacteria, the oxygen we depend on started appearing in earth's atmosphere.

MORE ABOUT

SUPER SCIENTIST

Real name: Maxwell J. Axiom
Hometown: Seattle, Washington
Height: 6' 1"   **Weight:** 192 lbs
Eyes: Brown   **Hair:** None

Super capabilities: Super intelligence; able to shrink to the size of an atom; sunglasses give x-ray vision; lab coat allows for travel through time and space.

Origin: Since birth, Max Axiom seemed destined for greatness. His mother, a marine biologist, taught her son about the mysteries of the sea. His father, a nuclear physicist and volunteer park ranger, schooled Max on the wonders of earth and sky.

One day on a wilderness hike, a megacharged lightning bolt struck Max with blinding fury. When he awoke, Max discovered a newfound energy and set out to learn as much about science as possible. He traveled the globe earning degrees in every aspect of the field. Upon his return, he was ready to share his knowledge and new identity with the world. He had become Max Axiom, Super Scientist.

GLOSSARY

antibiotic (an-ti-bye-OT-ik) — a drug that kills bacteria and is used to cure infections and disease

bacilli (bah-SILL-ee) — rod-shaped bacteria

binary fission (BYE-ner-ee FI-shuhn) — form of reproduction where the DNA is copied and the bacteria splits into two cells

cell (SEL) — the smallest unit of a living thing

cocci (KAH-kye) — ball-shaped bacteria

decomposer (dee-kuhm-PO-zur) — a living thing that turns dead things into food for others

DNA (dee en AY) — the genetic material that carries all of the instructions to make a living thing and keep it working; DNA stands for deoxyribonucleic acid.

eukaryotic cell (u-kare-ee-AH-tik SEL) — a cell that has DNA enclosed in a nucleus

flagellum (flah-GEL-luhm) — a whiplike tail that helps bacteria move

immune system (i-MYOON SISS-tuhm) — the part of the body that protects against germs and diseases

microorganism (mye-kroh-OR-guh-niz-uhm) — a living thing too small to be seen without a microscope

prokaryotic cell (pro-kare-ee-AH-tik SEL) — a cell that does not have a nucleus

spirilla (spuh-RILL-ah) — spiral-shaped bacteria

vaccine (vak-SEEN) — dead or weakened germs injected into a person or animal to help fight disease

READ MORE

Brunelle, Lynn, and Barbara Ravage. *Bacteria: Discovery Channel School Science*. Milwaukee, Wis.: Gareth Stevens Publishing, 2003.

Farrell, Jeanette. *Invisible Allies: Microbes That Shape Our Lives*. New York: Farrar, Straus, and Giroux, 2005.

Nye, Bill. *Bill Nye the Science Guy's Great Big Book of Tiny Germs*. New York: Hyperion Books for Children, 2005.

Romanek, Trudee. *Achoo! The Most Interesting Book You'll Ever Read About Germs*. Tonawanda, N.Y.: Kids Can Press, 2003.

Walker, Richard. *Microscopic Life*. Boston: Kingfisher, 2004.

INTERNET SITES

FactHound offers a safe, fun way to find Internet sites related to this book. All sites on FactHound have been researched by our staff.

Here's all you do:

Visit *www.facthound.com*

FactHound will fetch the best sites for you!

INDEX